TEAM TOOTS

A PICKLEBALL FART STORY

ISBN 9798867153328

Harvey the Heart and his best buddy Sue
were searching for something exciting to do.

They zoomed through the city and rode through the park,
but nothing was lighting their eyes with a spark.

They almost gave up when they heard a new sound,
then tooted with glee at the site that they found.
The players were bounding all over the court,
laughing while playing a new racket sport.

"It can't be tennis, those rackets are small."

"It can't be ping-pong, look at that ball!"

"Hey Harvey! Hey Suzie! You want to join in?"
Ollie the Octagon called with a grin.
"It's called pickleball - though I don't know why.
It's really of fun; you guys should try!"

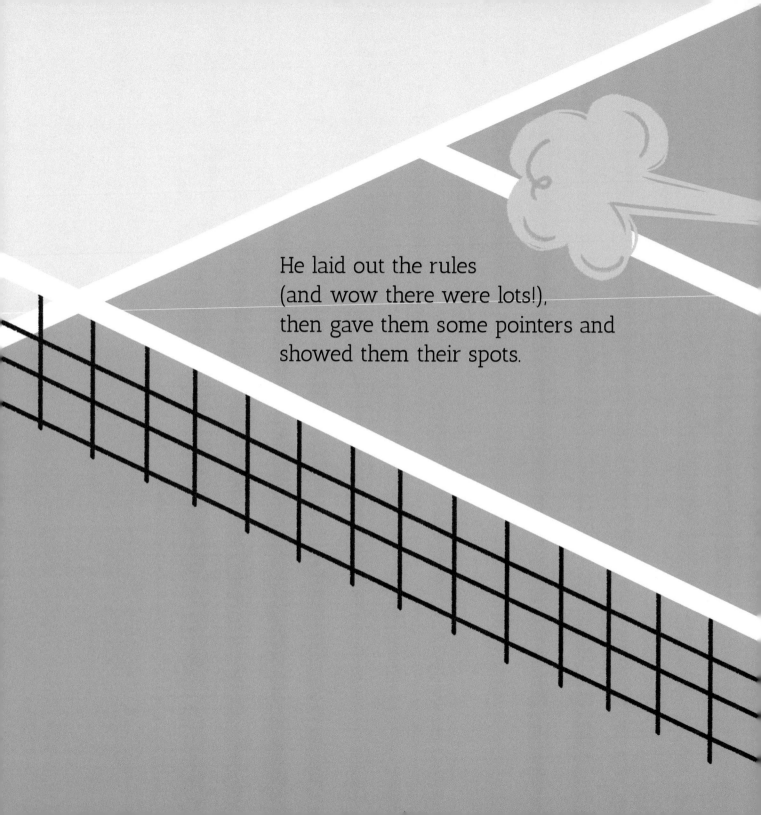

He laid out the rules
(and wow there were lots!),
then gave them some pointers and
showed them their spots.

"You've got to be able to
zip really fast."
"No worries," they laughed.
"We know how to blast."

"You'll need lots of skills for your pickleball spree.
Small hits called dinks and good teamwork are key."
They chirped, "Sure, we got it!" and waved him away,
too antsy to listen and eager to play.

Their very first game had them sprinting around
and it wasn't too long 'till they crashed to the ground.
"Hey Suzie Circle - that ball was mine!"
"No way Harvey Heart, can you see this line?"

Their second attempt didn't get any better.
Sue tried to make plays but he just wouldn't let her.
He blasted his bum and attacked every pass.
Poor Suzie was whiffing the ball AND his gas!

"This game is so frustrating!" Harvey Heart cried,
"Maybe we'd win if Sue actually tried."

"Oh, I'm the big problem? You won't let me dink!"
Harvey exploded!

"Well I can't improve if you won't let me hit,"
she slumped as she sniffled and whispered, "I quit."

Harvey felt just about two inches tall.
It wasn't her fault that he hogged every ball.

"Oh Suzie, I'm sorry! What was I thinking?
That's no way to treat your best friend or her dinking!
Can you forgive me? Please, will you stay?
I'll learn how to work as a team while we play."

Suzie agreed and they started out slow,
taking their time to get into a flow.
With practice and patience, they made quite a pair,
and soon they could smash every ball in the air.

"You can take this one!"
"What a great slice!"
"Watch out for the lob!"
"That fart dart was nice!"

They sailed through the courts on their flatulent steam,
finally playing the game as a team.
They learned how to block and to volley and spin,
and with their new skills...

...they were ready to win!

Made in the USA
Monee, IL
23 December 2024